EASY CRAFTS
for Kids

Cindy Groom Harry® and Staff, Designs & Consultation

PUBLICATIONS INTERNATIONAL, LTD.

Cindy Groom Harry is an author, crafts designer, and industry consultant whose work has been widely published in her own numerous craft books, and through hundreds of articles that have appeared in publications including *One-Hour Christmas Crafts For Kids, Better Homes and Gardens, McCall's Needlework and Crafts,* and *Craftworks for the Home.* She is a member of the Society of Craft Designers, where she previously served on the board of directors, and has also taught and demonstrated her designs on television craft programs.

Photography by Sacco Productions Limited/Chicago
Photographer: Cindy Trim
Photo Stylist: Missy Sacco
Photo Shoot Production: Roberta Ellis
Illustrations by Cindy Groom Harry® and Staff, Designs & Consultation
Aria Model & Talent Management, Ltd.: Charles Alex Belt III, Alyssa Hronec
Royal Model Management: Rachel Buchanan, Jessica Vilchis, Hector Zapata, Jr.

The mention of any product is merely a record of the procedure used and does not constitute an endorsement by the respective proprietors of Publications International, Ltd., nor does it constitute an endorsement by any of these companies that their products should be used in the manner recommended by this publication.

SOURCE OF MATERIALS

The following products were used in this book:

Aleene's™ Tack-It Over & Over: 54; **Aleene's™ Tacky Glue:** 6, 12, 21, 32, 54; **Aleene's Stick Glue:** 19, 44; **Black & Decker® 2 Temp™ Glue Gun:** 9, 12, 16, 19 22, 26, 27, 32, 36, 42, 44, 48, 54; **Black & Decker® 2 Temp™ Glue Sticks:** 9, 12, 16, 19, 22, 26, 27, 32, 36, 42, 44, 48, 54; **Crafty's Featherworks Feathers:** 39, 44, 54; **DecoArt™ Americana™ Acrylic Spray Sealer:** 9; **Delta Ceramcoat™ Paint:** 9, 16, 21, 32, 36, 48, 54; **Duncan Scribbles® Dimensional Paint:** 12, 16, 21, 36, 39, 44, 48; **Duncan Scribbles® Outline Pen:** 21; **The Felters Co. Craft 100® Felt:** 21; **Fiskars® Craft Snip:** 44, 54; **Fiskars® for Kids:** 21; **Fiskars® Pinking Shears:** 19; **Fiskars® Scissors for Kids:** 6, 12, 19, 22, 27, 32, 36, 42, 44, 48, 51, 54; **FloraCraft Blue Jay Chenille Stems:** 27, 32, 44, 48; **FloraCraft Blue Jay Jumbo Loopy Chenille:** 26, 36; **Forster™ Woodsies:** 16, 36; **Forster™ Wooden Dowels:** 36; **Hygloss Paper Doilies:** 32; **Hygloss Super Glossy Paper:** 19; **Hygloss Super Glossy Posterboard:** 19, 39, 44; **Kunin/Foss Felt:** 6, 12, 26, 32, 36, 39, 48, 54; **Magnetic Specialty, Inc. CraftMagic Magnetic Sheeting:** 42; **Magnetic Specialty, Inc. Magnetic Tape:** 6, 21; **One & Only Creations Mini Curl™ Curly Hair™:** 32; **Silver Brush, Ltd., Silverwhite™ Paint Brushes:** 9, 16, 21, 32, 36, 48, 54; **Speedball® Painters® Paint Markers:** 9; **Spinrite Plastic Canvas Yarn:** 21, 36, 39, 44, 51; **Teters Floral Products, Inc. Silk Flowers:** 27; **Teters Floral Products, Inc. Gypsophilia:** 48; **Wang's International, Inc.® Puffy Shapes:** 16; **Wrights® Eyelet Lace:** 22, 27; **Wrights® Picot Ribbon:** 22, 32; **Wrights® Rick Rack:** 44; **Wrights® Satin Ribbon:** 6, 26, 27; **X-ACTO® Craft Tweezer:** 22, 26, 36, 42, 44.

CONTENTS

Introduction

Dear parents and teachers—

We know that most kids will be able to make the projects with little help, but there will be times when your assistance is needed. If the child has never used a glue gun, explain that the nozzle and freshly applied glue is warm, even when set on low. Have a glass of water nearby just in case warm fingers need cooling. Occasionally, instructions direct the child to ask for adult help. Be sure everyone understands the "Important things to know" section found on pages 6 and 7. The general directions concerning patterns contain important instructions as well.

Most important, this should be an enjoyable, creative experience. Although we provide specific instructions, it's wonderful to see children create their own versions using their own ideas. ENJOY!

Hey kids—

With *Easy Crafts for Kids,* you can make any rainy day fun! This book will show you how to make great presents for mom or dad, a dynamite dinosaur magnet for your room, super snazzy sneakers to wear, and much, much more. There is something for everyone in this book!

Easy Crafts for Kids was made with you in mind. Many of the projects are fun things you can make by yourself. However, with some projects, you will need to ask an adult for help. It's a good idea to make a project following the instructions exactly. Then feel free to make another, using your imagination to change colors or designs to make it more your own. Think of all the variations you can make and all the gifts you can give!

Most important, HAVE FUN! Think how proud you'll be to say, "I made this myself!"

Key

Each project has been tested to measure the challenge level it presents to the crafter. The chart below shows you the key to the levels. Look for these apple symbols below the title of each project.

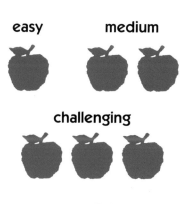

easy

medium

challenging

General pattern instructions

When the instructions for a project tell you to cut out a shape according to the pattern, begin by tracing the pattern from the book onto typing paper with a pencil. If the pattern has an arrow with the word FOLD next to a line, it is a half-pattern. Fold a sheet of typing paper in half and open up the paper. Place the fold line of the typing paper exactly on top of the fold line of the pattern and trace the pattern. Then refold and cut along the line, going through both layers of paper. Open paper for the full pattern.

A few of the patterns will have to be enlarged before cutting. This can be done at any print shop or photocopy center. The percentage of enlargement is clearly marked on each pattern. To attach a pattern to felt, roll two-inch lengths of masking tape into circles with the adhesive side out. Attach the tape rolls to the back of the pattern in several places. Place pattern onto felt and cut through both paper and felt layers along the lines. If you are using a half-pattern, open the pattern and tape the full pattern to the felt. Cut on the edge of the pattern lines.

Important things to know!

Although we know you'll want to get started right away, please read these basic steps before beginning:

1. Go through the book and decide what project you want to make first.

Read the materials list and the instructions completely.

2. Gather all your materials, remembering to ask permission! If you need to purchase materials, take along your book or make a shopping list so you know exactly what you need.

3. Prepare your work area ahead of time. Cleanup will be easier if you prepare first!

4. Be sure that an adult is nearby to help if you need it.

5. Be careful not to put any materials near your mouth. Watch out for small items, like beads, around kids and pets.

6. Use the glue gun set on the low temperature setting,

unless the directions tell you to put it on high. Do not touch the nozzle or freshly applied glue, because they may still be hot. Use the glue gun with adult permission only!

7. Wear an apron when painting with acrylic paints, because after the paint dries, it is permanent. If you do get it on your clothes, wash with soap and warm water immediately.

8. When the instructions direct you to paint two coats of a color, let the first coat dry before painting the second.

9. Clean up afterwards, and put away all materials and tools.

Take a minute to look at the pictures below. In the materials section for each project, you will find pictures of these frequently used items in addition to the other supplies needed.

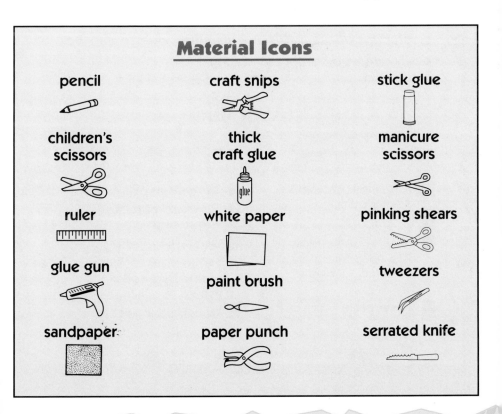

Material Icons

pencil

children's scissors

ruler

glue gun

sandpaper

craft snips

thick craft glue

white paper

paint brush

paper punch

stick glue

manicure scissors

pinking shears

tweezers

serrated knife

Snowman Sweatshirt

Who says you need snow to build a snowman? Expand your winter wardrobe by turning an ordinary sweatshirt into a work of wearable art. Accented with glittering crystal snowflakes, this eye-catching design can be easily removed before laundering.

Materials

- Dimensional paint: black, glittering crystal
- Red sweatshirt
- Felt: 8 × 10 inches white, 2 × 4 inches black, 1 × 3 inches red, 1 × 2 inches pink
- 2 green poms, ¾-inch each

- 2 wiggle eyes, 10mm each
- 4 black half-ball buttons, ⁵⁄₁₆-inch each
- 2-inch yellow feather
- 14-inch length of ⅝-inch-wide red/green plaid ribbon
- Repositionable glue

1 Randomly squeeze-paint glittering crystal snowflakes on shirt front by painting a one-inch horizontal line and one-inch vertical line forming a cross, and ¾-inch diagonal lines forming an x on top of cross. Let paint dry. Repeat on shirt back.

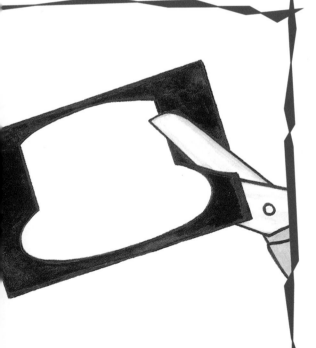

2 Using patterns on pages 94 and 95, trace and cut snowman base, bottom, middle, head, and two arms from white felt; hat from black felt; hat band from red felt; and two cheeks from pink felt.

3 Using craft glue, attach parts to snowman base in the following order: bottom, middle, head, arms, hat, and hat band. Use glue gun on low temperature to attach ear muffs, cheeks, and wiggle eyes as shown. Squeeze-paint black mouth from cheek to cheek. Cut shanks off buttons with craft snip. Use one button for nose, gluing remaining three buttons down middle of snowman. Tuck and glue end of feather under hatband. For scarf, glue ends of two 7-inch lengths of ribbon to base at snowman's neckline. Wrap ribbon lengths around front and knot.

4 Turn over snowman and apply two or three coats of repositionable glue according to manufacturer's instructions. Let dry 24 hours and attach snowman to upper right front of shirt.

Dad's Key Keeper

Unlock your imagination and help Dad be better organized with this handsome key rack, perfect for hanging in the kitchen, front hallway, or at work. It's a lot easier to make than it looks. Coins, charms, and medallions are the "key" ingredients for this project.

Materials

- 5 × 7-inch wood plaque
- Light blue acrylic paint
- Bright blue paint marker
- Acrylic spray sealer
- Old newspapers

- 3 gold cup hooks, ½-inch each
- 10 assorted coins, charms, and medallions, between ½ and 1½ inches
- 2 soda can tabs

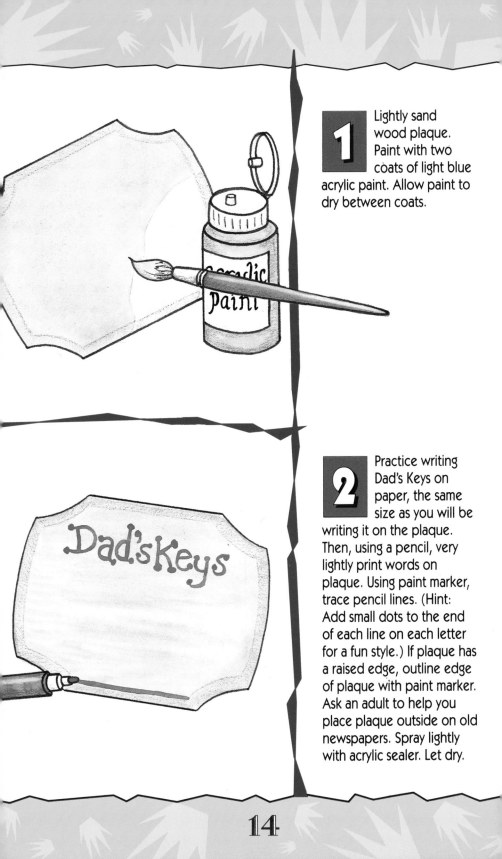

1 Lightly sand wood plaque. Paint with two coats of light blue acrylic paint. Allow paint to dry between coats.

2 Practice writing Dad's Keys on paper, the same size as you will be writing it on the plaque. Then, using a pencil, very lightly print words on plaque. Using paint marker, trace pencil lines. (Hint: Add small dots to the end of each line on each letter for a fun style.) If plaque has a raised edge, outline edge of plaque with paint marker. Ask an adult to help you place plaque outside on old newspapers. Spray lightly with acrylic sealer. Let dry.

Dad's Keys

3 Ask an adult to help you screw the three cup hooks into wood, evenly spaced, about one inch up from bottom of plaque. Arrange trinkets and use the glue gun (set on low) to glue pieces to plaque. Turn glue gun to high and wait a few minutes before next step.

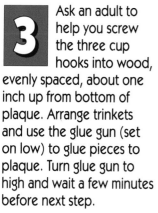

4 To hang plaque, glue two soda can tabs to back of plaque so that loops of tabs will hang on nails in wall.

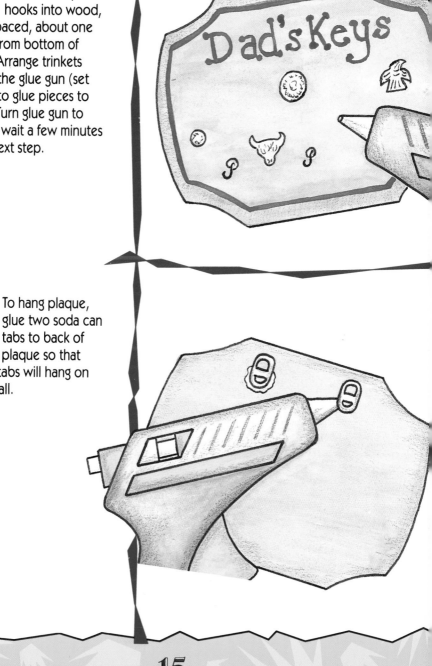

Puppet Puppy

Don't worry—it barks sometimes, but it never bites. Even if you can't have a dog where you live, you can still have this cute little puppet puppy to call your own. All you need are the basic materials listed below. The doghouse is optional.

Materials

- Felt: two 9 × 12 inches white, 5 × 6 inches black, 6 × 8 inches brown, 1-inch square red, 1 × 3 inches` royal blue
- Poms: 1½-inch beige, ½-inch black
- 2 wiggle eyes, 15mm each
- Black dimensional paint
- 2½-inch dog biscuit

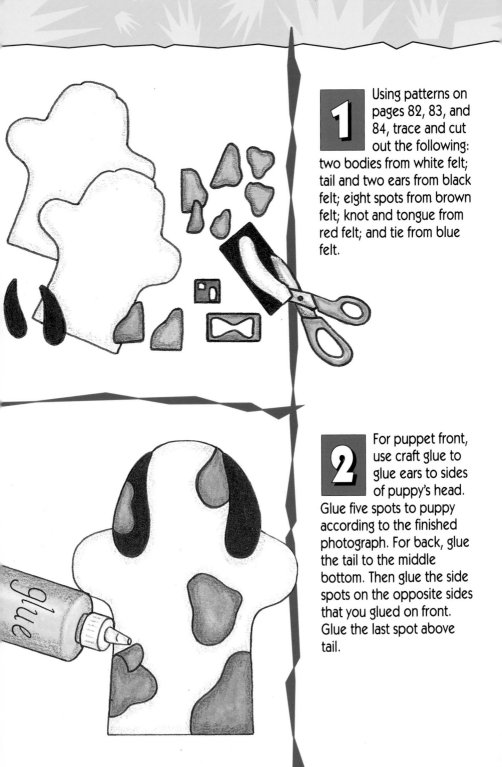

1 Using patterns on pages 82, 83, and 84, trace and cut out the following: two bodies from white felt; tail and two ears from black felt; eight spots from brown felt; knot and tongue from red felt; and tie from blue felt.

2 For puppet front, use craft glue to glue ears to sides of puppy's head. Glue five spots to puppy according to the finished photograph. For back, glue the tail to the middle bottom. Then glue the side spots on the opposite sides that you glued on front. Glue the last spot above tail.

glue

3 For muzzle, glue 1½-inch pom to middle of puppy's face. Glue ½-inch pom to top front of muzzle for nose. Glue straight end of tongue into the lower side of muzzle pom. Glue wiggle eyes to face just above muzzle. Glue knot to center of bow tie. Glue bow tie just below tongue.

4 To assemble puppet, use glue gun (set on low). Match up front and back pieces (make sure the decorated sides face outward). Lift up puppet front. Apply line of glue a few inches at a time around edge of puppet; be sure to leave bottom open.

5 Squeeze-paint black paw lines on left paw; let dry. Glue dog biscuit to puppy's right paw.

Soldier Magnet

Here's a project that's highly ranked! This magnetized soldier figure, which can be used to post the day's orders or as simple decoration, commands a lot of attention with its blue-and-red tailoring and golden trimmings.

Materials

- 2 × 6-inch cardboard
- Felt: 2 × 6 inches blue, 2 square inches red, 1 × 2 inches beige, 1 × 2 inches black
- 3-inch length of 2mm gold cord
- Dimensional paint: black and glittering gold

- 1-inch length of ½-inch-wide gold braid
- Pink acrylic paint
- Black fine line felt tip marker
- 2-inch length black yarn
- 3-inch length magnetic strip

Christmas List
Mom - Christmas
Dad - Socks a
Sis - Tree sur
Nickey - Soldier
Misha - Angel
Aunt Mary - Ca
Ms. Brody - te
* Make ca

1 Using the pattern on page 96, trace and cut the soldier from the cardboard and the blue felt. Apply glue to the cardboard, and attach the felt soldier to the top of the cardboard soldier.

2 Using the patterns on page 96, trace and cut the jacket from the red felt, the head and hands from the beige felt, and the shoes and cap bill from the black felt. Apply glue to the jacket, hands, head, and shoes. Position these glued pieces into place on the felt soldier. Apply glue to the straight edge of the cap bill, and attach it to the area just above the head.

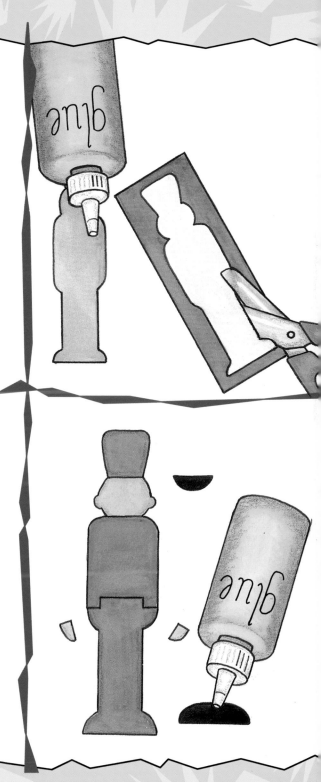

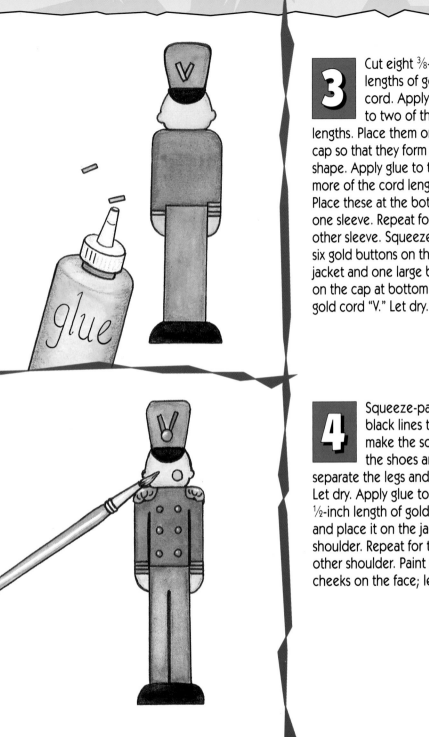

3 Cut eight ⅜-inch lengths of gold cord. Apply glue to two of the cord lengths. Place them on the cap so that they form a "V" shape. Apply glue to three more of the cord lengths. Place these at the bottom of one sleeve. Repeat for the other sleeve. Squeeze-paint six gold buttons on the jacket and one large button on the cap at bottom of gold cord "V." Let dry.

4 Squeeze-paint black lines to make the soles of the shoes and to separate the legs and arms. Let dry. Apply glue to a ½-inch length of gold braid, and place it on the jacket shoulder. Repeat for the other shoulder. Paint pink cheeks on the face; let dry.

5 Use a marker to draw the eyes, eyebrows, nose, and mouth. For the hair, glue two ½-inch lengths of yarn to the side of the head underneath the cap bill. Trim the yarn so it just covers the top of the ears. Repeat with the other side of the head. Remove the paper from the adhesive side of the magnetic strip, and attach the magnet to the back of the soldier.

Snazzy Sneaker Set

Here's a project that will have everyone around you seeing stars. You'll need more than 50 of them to become an official member of the Snazzy Sneaker Set.

Materials

- White sneakers
- 26 red puffy stars, ¾-inch each
- 27 blue puffy stars, ¾-inch each
- White painter's cap
- Glittering silver dimensional paint
- 2 (size H) wood circles, ¾-inch each
- White acrylic paint
- 2 earring backs

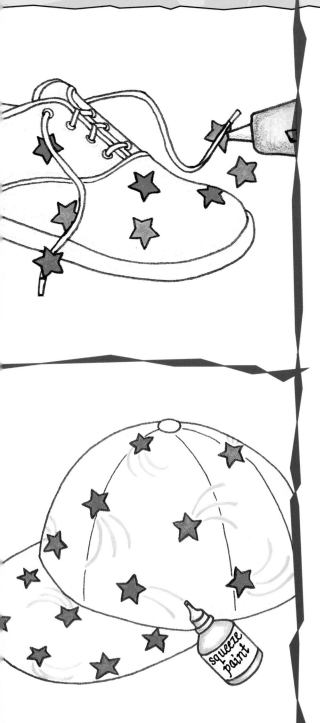

1 Plan how to arrange five red and six blue stars on one shoe according to the finished photos. Apply glue (use low temperature) to back of each star, and place on shoe. Align and glue together two red puffy stars back to back just below the end of one shoelace, sandwiching shoelace between the stars. Repeat with two blue puffy stars for the other end of the shoelace. Repeat for second shoe. Similarly, position and glue ten blue and eleven red stars on painter's cap.

2 Squeeze-paint three glittering silver rays shooting out from each star on shoes and painter's cap. Let paint dry.

3 For earring, paint wood circle with two coats of white paint. Let paint dry between coats. Apply glue to back of blue puffy star and place on wood circle. Apply glue to center back of wood circle and place one of the earring backs into glue. Repeat to make second earring with red puffy star.

Trick-or-Treat Bag

You probably went to a lot of trouble to get a great Halloween costume this year. Why not make a great bag to go with it? Here's a fun design that combines two traditional symbols—a ghost and a jack-o'-lantern.

Materials

- Brown grocery bag (6½ × 10-inch base, at least 12 inches high)
- Shiny paper: 9-inch square white, 9-inch square orange, 2 × 3-inch yellow, 2-inch square green, 2 × 3-inch black

- Black permanent felt-tipped marker
- 1½ × 18 inches white posterboard
- 52-inch length of 1½-inch-wide Halloween print craft ribbon
- 2 sheets black tissue paper

1 Use ruler to measure paper sack to 12 inches high. Cut along line with pinking shears.

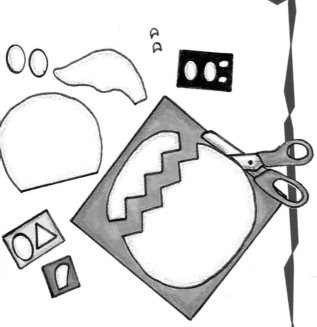

2 Using patterns on pages 86, 87, and 88, trace and cut the following: ghost head, arm, eye crescents, and jack-o'-lantern eyes from white shiny paper; jack-o'-lantern and top from orange shiny paper; jack-o'-lantern nose and mouth from yellow shiny paper; stem from green shiny paper; and jack-o'-lantern pupils and ghost eye from black shiny paper.

3 Referring to photo, position parts on work-table in the following order: ghost head, arm, jack-o'-lantern top, stem, head, eyes and pupils, nose, mouth, black ghost eyes, and eye crescents. Use stick glue to assemble. Using a black marker, draw eyebrows and mouth on ghost and eyebrows on pumpkin (see finished photograph). Use stick glue to glue entire jack-o'-lantern/ghost piece to the front of the bag.

4 To make handle, use a glue gun (set on low) to glue one inch of posterboard strip to the top outside middle of the short side of the bag. Repeat on other side of bag with other end of posterboard strip. Glue one end of ribbon to bottom middle of bag, spot-gluing as you go up side of bag, across posterboard strip, down other side, and across middle of bottom until overlapping other end. Tuck two sheets of black tissue paper inside bag.

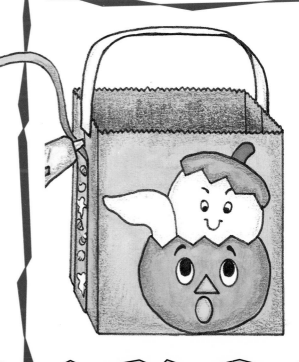

Lion Pencil Topper

Kids love lions, so this simple beginner's project is sure to have your little ones roaring with approval. It's also a perfect example of how simple, everyday objects can be transformed into something special.

Materials

- New pencil
- Poms: 2-inch gold, two ½-inch yellow, ¼-inch black
- 7-inch length yellow jumbo loopy chenille

- Felt: ½ × 1-inch gold, ½-inch square red
- 2 wiggle eyes, 8mm each
- 10-inch length of ¼-inch-wide purple satin ribbon

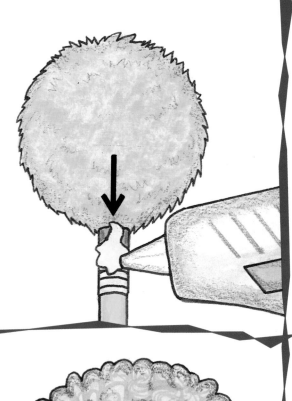

1 Apply glue to top and sides of pencil eraser, and insert into two-inch gold pom, pushing sides of the pom into the glue on the sides of the eraser (use low temperature and be careful; glue can be hot!).

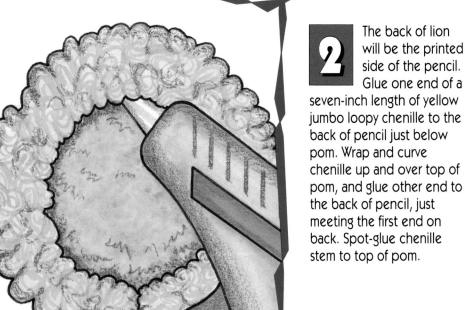

2 The back of lion will be the printed side of the pencil. Glue one end of a seven-inch length of yellow jumbo loopy chenille to the back of pencil just below pom. Wrap and curve chenille up and over top of pom, and glue other end to the back of pencil, just meeting the first end on back. Spot-glue chenille stem to top of pom.

3 Using patterns on page 90, trace and cut tongue from red felt and two ears from gold felt (or substitute two ½-inch gold poms for ears, as shown in illustration). Refer to the finished photograph for placement of pieces. Glue ears to pom where mane and pom meet. For jowls, glue two ½-inch yellow poms to face just below center. Glue tongue below and between jowls. For nose, glue black pom at top middle of jowls. Use tweezers to glue wiggle eyes to face so bottom edges of wiggle eyes touch top of jowls. Spot-glue eyes to jowls to hold.

4 Wrap the purple satin ribbon around pencil just below pom and tie a bow. Spot-glue ribbon to pencil.

Lace-n-Flowers Barrette

ilk flowers and satin ribbons highlight this beautiful pink-and-white barrette. This lovely fashion accessory can easily be coordinated with a spring or summer wardrobe.

Materials

- White thread
- Sewing needle
- 14-inch length of 2-inch-wide white eyelet lace
- ¼-inch-wide satin ribbon: 27-inch length white, 27-inch length pink

- 2 inches white slim chenille stem
- 3 pink silk rosebuds, 1 inch each
- 6 pink silk flowers, ¾-inch each
- 2¾-inch barrette

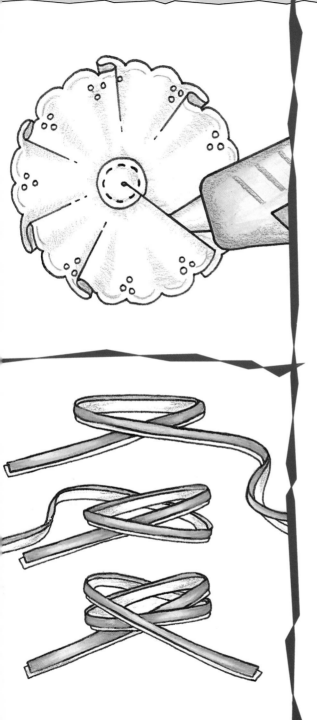

1 Thread needle and knot ends of thread. Stitch ½-inch-long basting stitches through binding edge of eyelet lace. Pull thread tightly to form circle of eyelet lace and knot. Cut thread. Slightly overlap ends of lace and glue together (use glue gun on low).

2 Match pink and white ribbon ends together. Form a bow with four loops (double bow), then wrap the chenille stem around the center of the bow; twist ends together at back. Fold over twisted ends. Glue center of bow to center of eyelet lace circle.

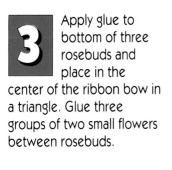

3 Apply glue to bottom of three rosebuds and place in the center of the ribbon bow in a triangle. Glue three groups of two small flowers between rosebuds.

4 Apply a line of glue to top of barrette and place back of eyelet lace circle onto barrette.

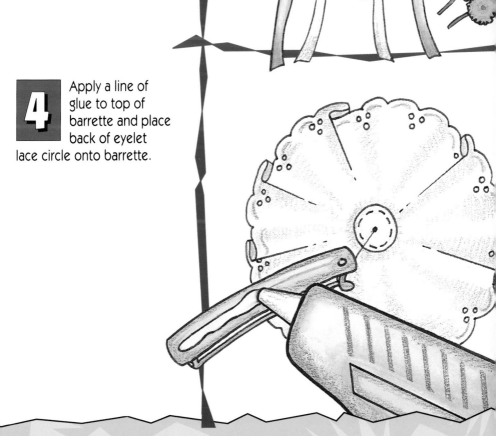

Doily Angel

This lacy version of a seraph is a vision in pure white. Adorned with blue satin ribbon and a gold tinsel halo, she is ready to take her place on any yuletide fireplace mantle or dinner table. The effect is sure to be heavenly.

Materials

- 2 pieces white felt, 9 × 12 inches each
- 2 white paper doilies: a 12-inch and an 8-inch doily
- 2-inch hard-pressed foam ball
- Acrylic paint: beige, pink
- Black permanent felt-tipped marker
- Small amount mini-curl blonde hair
- 12-inch length gold tinsel stem
- 12-inch length of ⅜-inch-wide light blue picot satin ribbon

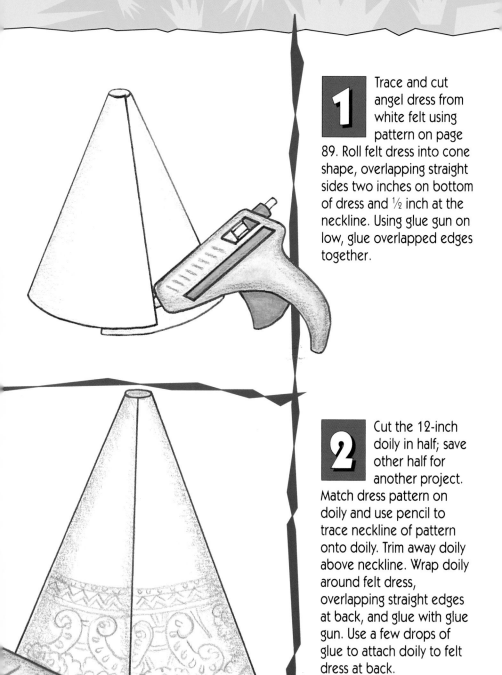

1 Trace and cut angel dress from white felt using pattern on page 89. Roll felt dress into cone shape, overlapping straight sides two inches on bottom of dress and ½ inch at the neckline. Using glue gun on low, glue overlapped edges together.

2 Cut the 12-inch doily in half; save other half for another project. Match dress pattern on doily and use pencil to trace neckline of pattern onto doily. Trim away doily above neckline. Wrap doily around felt dress, overlapping straight edges at back, and glue with glue gun. Use a few drops of glue to attach doily to felt dress at back.

3 Trace and cut angel wing from white felt using pattern on page 90. Roll felt wing into cone shape, overlapping straight edges one inch at bottom of wing and tapering to a point at the top. Glue. Cut the eight-inch doily in half. Wrap doily around wing, overlapping straight edges at side seam, and glue. Attach doily to felt wing at side seam. Apply glue to side seam of wing and place at side of dress. Repeat with second wing.

4 For head, lightly sand foam ball. Paint with two coats of beige. Let dry. Using glue gun, apply glue to neckline of dress and place head into glue. For hair, apply craft glue to top, sides, and back of head. Gently fluff curly hair and place into glue, slightly overlapping curls. Spot-glue and add more hair as needed. Paint pink cheeks on face; let dry. Use marker to draw eyes, eyebrows, nose, and mouth (see finished photograph).

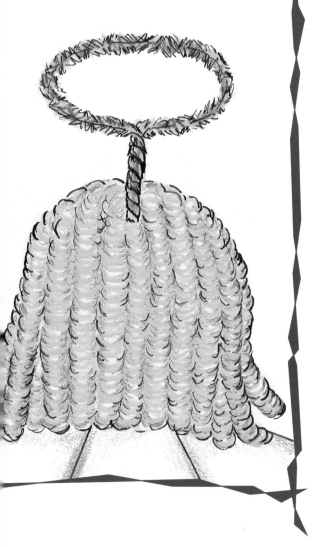

5 For halo, make a two-inch-wide circle in the middle of the ten-inch length of glitter stem. Twist ends together. Insert and glue (with craft glue) twisted ends into back top of angel's head. Tie the ribbon into a bow. Glue to center front of neckline.

Race Car Magnet

Vrooom! Your kids will speed through their chores—or at least keep better track of them—once they get equipped with this flashy race car magnet. It's good for tacking up all kinds of notes and reminders—just what today's busy youngsters need to keep ahead of the pack!

Materials

Magnetic sheeting: 3×8 inches red, 2×3 inches black, $1\frac{1}{2} \times 2$ inches gold, 4 inches orange, $\frac{3}{4} \times 2$ inches blue, $\frac{3}{4} \times 1\frac{1}{2}$ inches white

Math Test
on
Friday!

Camp out
at Johnny'?
on
Saturday !!

SUPER

Chores

Clean my room

Return library book

Take out the Garbage

Feed the Dog

Finish Homework

1 Trace and cut the pieces from magnetic sheeting using patterns on page 85. Use regular scissors for most cutting and manicure scissors for small curves. Cut the car in red; front and back tires and visor in black; front and back wheels and exhaust pipe in gold; body flame in orange; helmet and engine in blue; and window in white.

2 Assemble pieces, using the red car as the backing and gluing pieces to it in the order listed in Step 1 (see photograph).

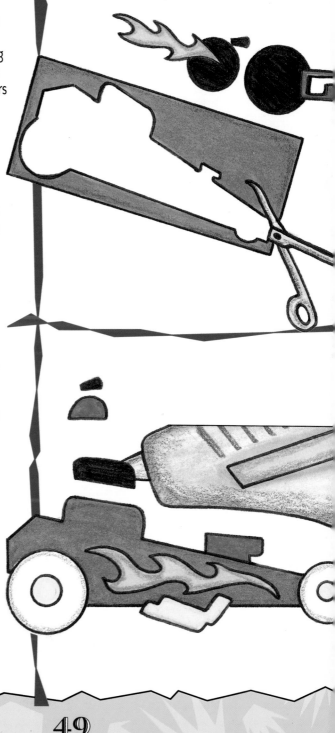

Bunny Plant Poke

Don't be alarmed when this comical carrot-nibbler pokes its cute little head out of your favorite floral arrangement. Made of chenille, felt, and poms, this design incorporates wiggle eyes and floppy ears.

Materials

- 12-inch length white jumbo loopy chenille
- 18-inch length of 5mm wooden dowel
- 1 white pom, 2 inches
- 2 white poms, ½-inch each
- 1 pink pom, ¼ inch
- 1 white pom, 1 inch
- Felt: 3½ × 5 inches white, 2-inch square pink
- 2 wiggle eyes, 10mm each
- Black dimensional paint
- 1½-inch wood teardrop shape (E)
- Orange acrylic paint
- 9-inch length green yarn

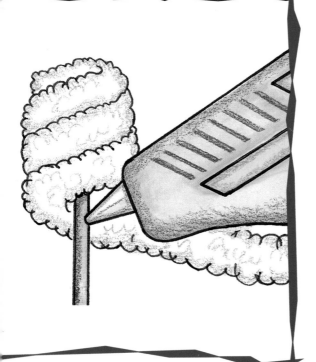

1 Spiral-wrap 12-inch length of chenille around 3 inches of one end of the dowel, spot-gluing every inch. (Be sure glue gun is on low.)

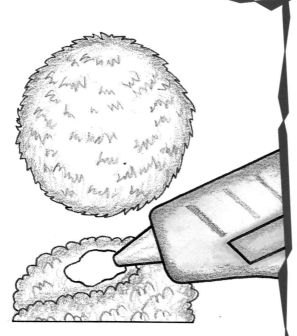

2 For head, apply glue in a circle (the size of a nickel) on top of the chenille and place two-inch white pom into glue. For jowls, glue two ½-inch white poms to bottom of head. For teeth, trace and cut teeth from white felt according to pattern on page 80; glue just under jowls. For nose, glue ¼-inch pink pom to the top middle of jowls. Using tweezers, glue two wiggle eyes so bottom edges are above top of jowls.

3 Trace and cut two white felt ears, two pink felt inner ears, and two white felt paws according to patterns on page 80. Glue pink inner ears to white felt ears and glue to top of head. Glue one-inch white pom to bottom left side of body for tail. Squeeze black dimensional paint lines on paw ends (see illustration). Let dry. Glue paws to sides, attaching points to neck.

4 Paint wooden teardrop shape orange; let dry. Cut green yarn into three 3-inch lengths. For carrot top, align ends of two lengths of green yarn and tie the third length around middle of them. Fold up all ends and glue knotted end to back top of carrot. Glue carrot in bunny's left paw. Insert dowel into potted plant.

Egg Critters

Depending on the materials your kids use and the colors they choose, these fanciful critters can be made to look like ducks or chickens or something in between. With an array of plastic eggs, colored feathers, and other essentials, their imaginations can truly soar!

Materials

- 2 × 3 inches white posterboard
- Felt: 2 × 4 inches orange, ¾ × 1¼ inches red, 1 × 2 inches purple
- Orange dimensional paint
- 2-inch yellow plastic egg
- 2-inch yellow pom
- Yarn: 14-inch length yellow, 12-inch length green
- 2 wiggle eyes, 10mm each
- Feathers (assorted colors): three 4-inch, two 2-inch

1 Trace and cut foot from posterboard and orange felt according to pattern on page 81. With glue gun on low, glue felt foot to posterboard foot. Squeeze orange dimensional paint lines on foot according to pattern; let dry. Repeat to make other foot. Position feet (felt side up) on work surface ¼ inch apart. Glue yellow plastic egg (rounded side) to feet.

2 For head, glue two-inch pom to top of egg. For hair, cut five 2-inch lengths of yellow yarn. Align ends of the five lengths. With the remaining four-inch length of yellow yarn, wrap around middle of two-inch lengths; tie a knot. Fold up all ends of yarn and trim ends to make even. Glue knotted end to top center of head. Wrap middle of 12-inch length of green yarn around bottom of yarn hairs and tie a bow. Trim tails.

3 Trace and cut beak from orange felt and tongue from red felt according to patterns on page 81. Glue tongue to inside center of beak and fold across middle according to patterns. Glue outside of fold to lower middle of face. Use tweezers to glue two wiggle eyes to head, just touching sides of beak.

4 Cut bow tie from purple felt according to pattern on page 81 and glue to egg just under beak. For tail feathers, glue four-inch feathers to lower back of egg. Glue two-inch feathers to sides of body for wings. Create your own birds by using different colored eggs, feathers, feet, hair, etc.

Petal Posies

Flowers have a way of brightening any occasion. These posies, constructed of felt with green chenille stems, are especially charming, since they're all handmade! Bunches of tiny gypsophila add a natural touch.

Materials

- Felt: 4 × 8 inches light blue, 4 × 8 inches lavender, 5 × 10 inches pink, 3½ × 9 inches green
- Green dimensional paint
- 2 white hard-pressed foam balls, 1¼ inches each
- Yellow acrylic paint
- Three lengths of green chenille stems, 8 inches each
- 30-inch length of 1-inch-wide colorful craft ribbon (to match flowers)
- 6-inch length chenille stem (color to match ribbon)
- Small amount natural gypsophila
- Small can tab

1 Trace and cut the following according to patterns on pages 92 and 93: two round flowers from light blue felt, two round flowers from lavender felt, two pointed flowers from pink felt, and six leaves from green felt. With adult help, use a serrated knife to cut foam balls in half. Paint halves with two coats of yellow acrylic paint, allowing to dry between coats. Glue flat side of ball half to center of felt flower. To give flowers a dimensional look, apply a line of glue around very bottom edge of foam ball and fold up petals around ball. Hold until set (be careful, glue can be hot!).

2 For stem, glue one inch of one end of an eight-inch length of chenille stem to center of one felt flower. Align edges of other felt flower of the same color on top of first, sandwiching chenille stem between. Apply a line of glue between layers ⅛ inch from edge a few inches at a time.

1 inch

3 Glue ¼ inch of one end of a leaf to a chenille stem. Repeat, adding two leaves to each of two other chenille stems for a total of five leaves on stems. Save one leaf for later. Squeeze-paint green lines on leaves for veins; let dry.

4 For bow, bend ribbon to form two 3-inch loops with 7-inch streamers. Pinch together middle of bow and wrap a six-inch length of a chenille stem around center. Add stems of gypsophila among the flower stems. Wrap chenille stem binder around all stems and twist ends together at back. Trim and fold over. Cut V-notches in streamers. Glue final leaf to top back of uppermost flower. Glue can tab to top middle of back to hang bouquet.

Plastic Canvas Bookmarks

Forget those dog-eared library books—or hunting for paper clips and scraps of paper! For your little bookworms, these indestructible plastic canvas markers are the perfect way to remember where they left off reading, at the same time showcasing their special interests.

Materials

red bookmark:

- Yarn: 60-inch length white, 84-inch length navy blue
- Large-eyed needle
- 2 × 6-inch piece red plastic canvas
- 4 red, white, and blue stickers (as shown or similar)

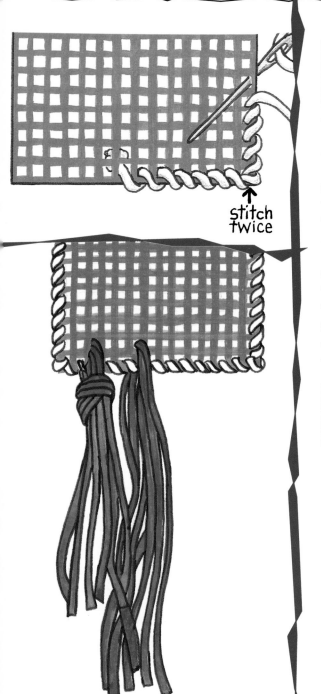

stitch twice

1 (Use desired color yarn and plastic canvas.) Tie a knot in one end of a 60-inch length yarn. Then knot again. Thread other end through the needle. Beginning at the middle small edge, insert needle from back and pull yarn through. Wrap yarn around edge and back up through next square. Continue stitching, placing needle through corner squares twice, one stitch on each side of the corner. Tie another double knot in other end at the back.

2 For tassels, cut 84-inch length of yarn into seven-inch lengths. Thread one seven-inch length into needle and go through the third square from the left in the hole above the border. Repeat with two more lengths in same hole. Align all yarn ends and tie a knot. Do the same, making three more tassels, but leaving two empty squares between each tassel.

3 Attach two stickers to bookmark front and two more to back.

Here are the materials you'll need to make the other bookmarks.

pink bookmark:

- Yarn: 60-inch length dark pink, 84-inch length turquoise
- Large-eyed needle
- 2 × 6-inch piece light pink plastic canvas
- 4 pink, purple, and turquoise stickers (as shown or similar)

green dinosaur bookmark:

- Yarn: 60-inch length white, 84-inch length purple
- Large-eyed needle
- 2 × 6-inch piece green plastic canvas
- 4 green, purple, and orange stickers (as shown or similar)

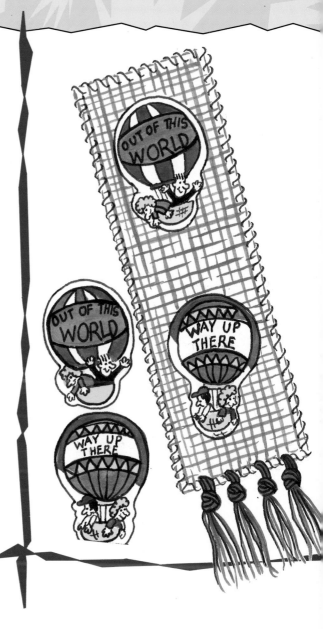

bring
lunch money
Tuesday for
field trip

Donald Dinosaur Magnet

Believe it or not, dinosaurs make great pets, especially magnetized ones like Donald. Attach him to your refrigerator or locker, and you can use him to hang up drawings, photos, or important reminders.

Materials

- 3 × 6 inches cardboard
- Felt: 3 × 6 inches green, 1-inch square pink
- Green poms: one 2-inch, ten ½-inch
- Black permanent felt-tipped marker
- 2 wiggle eyes, 7mm each
- 9-inch length of ¼-inch-wide purple satin ribbon
- 2-inch length of ½-inch-wide magnetic strip

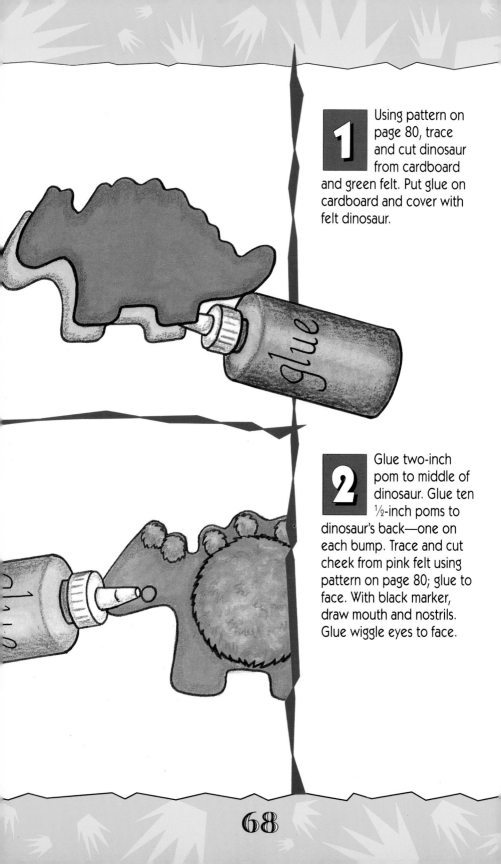

1 Using pattern on page 80, trace and cut dinosaur from cardboard and green felt. Put glue on cardboard and cover with felt dinosaur.

2 Glue two-inch pom to middle of dinosaur. Glue ten ½-inch poms to dinosaur's back—one on each bump. Trace and cut cheek from pink felt using pattern on page 80; glue to face. With black marker, draw mouth and nostrils. Glue wiggle eyes to face.

3 Cut off three inches of purple ribbon. Wrap this ribbon around dinosaur's neck, and glue overlapping ends on the back of the cardboard. Tie a bow with the remaining six inches of ribbon. Glue bow to ribbon around neck. Remove paper from adhesive side of magnetic strip and place on back of dinosaur.

Marvelous Masks

Who is that intriguing young woman in the multicolored mask? Or that mysterious fellow behind the spider web? Only their friends will know for sure when your kids don these cleverly constructed party masks. They're perfect for Halloween, for theme dances—any occasion where drama is part of the fun and games.

Materials

feather mask:
- 5-inch squares of tissue paper: blue, red, yellow, green
- 4 × 8 inches white posterboard

- 37-inch length yellow baby rickrack
- 14-inch length of ¼-inch-wide white elastic cord
- 6 feathers to match tissue paper, 2 to 4 inches long

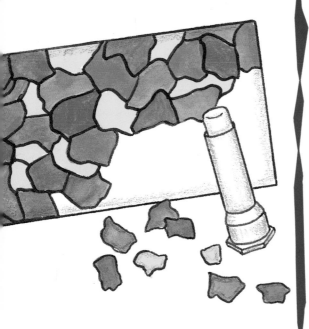

Feather Mask Instructions

1 Rip tissue paper into irregular ½-inch to 1¼-inch pieces. Apply stick glue to posterboard. Attach ripped pieces, overlapping edges and randomly placing colors until entire posterboard is covered. Turn over posterboard. Trace mask outline and eye holes onto posterboard using pattern from page 91. Cut on lines. Turn right side up.

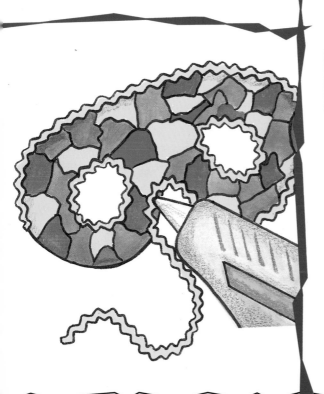

2 Use glue gun (on low) for the following: Glue five inches of rickrack, a few inches at a time, around each eye hole. Also, glue 27-inch length of rickrack around outside edge of mask. Paper-punch hole on each side of mask as indicated on pattern. Insert ends of 14-inch length elastic through holes and tie knots at back of mask—adjust as needed to fit your head. Spot-glue elastic knots to hold.

3 Glue ends of three feathers to back of mask as shown.

You'll need most of the same tools to make the spider mask.

spider mask:

☐ 4 × 8 inches orange posterboard

☐ Black dimensional paint

☐ 14-inch length of ¼-inch-wide white elastic cord

☐ 2 black poms, 1-inch each

☐ 2 black poms, ¾-inch each

☐ 4 wiggle eyes, 7mm each

☐ Two 12-inch lengths black chenille

☐ 22-inch length black yarn; 2 four-inch lengths black yarn

Spider Mask Instructions

1 Trace mask outline and eye holes onto back side of orange poster-board according to pattern on page 91. Cut on lines. Punch holes on sides where indicated. Lightly draw pencil web guidelines on front of mask according to spider pattern. Squeeze dimensional paint on web lines; let dry.

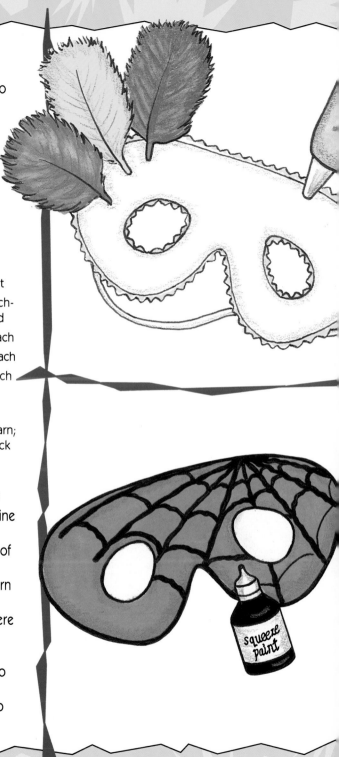

2 Glue together one-inch and ¾-inch black poms for spider's head and body. Use tweezers to glue two wiggle eyes to front of head. For legs, stack and glue middles of four 3-inch lengths of chenille stems. Glue body to top of leg stack. Bend legs down ½ inch on end of each leg. Bend out a ¼ inch on end for foot. Slightly flatten out legs. Repeat procedure to make another spider but do not flatten legs.

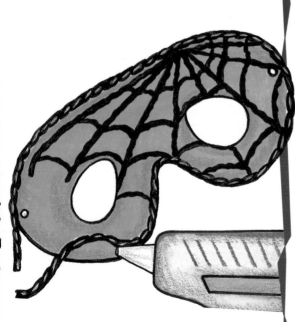

3 Leaving two inches unglued, begin gluing 22-inch length of yarn about ½ inch above left hole punch, continuing all the way around outside of mask. Glue first spider to top right of mask. Glue dangling end of yarn between second spider's head and body pom. Glue the 4-inch lengths of yarn around eye holes. Attach elastic cord as explained in Step 2 of the feather mask instructions.

Seed Heart Decoration

Incorporating seeds, beans, and other "natural" ingredients, this carefully assembled decorative piece makes a magnificent Valentine's Day gift. Not for beginners, this challenging project requires the ability to work with considerable precision. Can you do it?

Materials

- 6-inch square cardboard
- 43 pumpkin seeds
- 30 kidney beans
- 52 pinto beans
- 85 small pearl tapioca

- 58-inch length of ¼-inch-wide pink picot satin ribbon
- 22-inch length of 1-inch-wide white lace

NOTE: Because seed sizes vary, you may need more than we used. It is best to buy extras.

1 Using pattern on page 81, trace and cut heart from cardboard. Apply one inch of glue (use low temperature) to inside bottom of heart and use tweezers to place pumpkin seeds into glue, neatly in a row, with each seed slightly overlapping the last. Continue around inside of heart, gluing one inch at a time until reaching the bottom again.

2 Repeat gluing with two or three more rows of the other seeds (kidney beans, pinto beans, small pearl tapioca). Look at finished photograph for ideas.

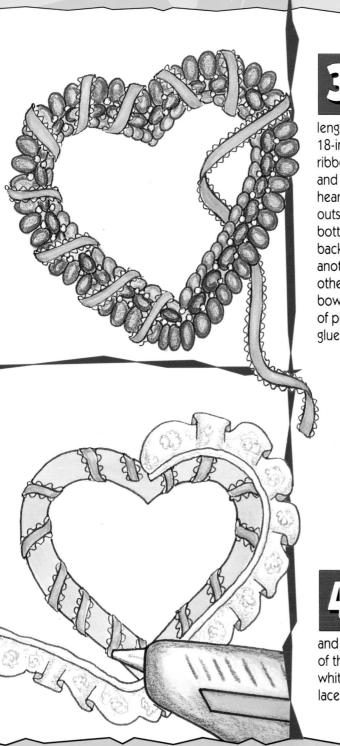

3 From pink picot ribbon, cut two 18-inch lengths and one 12-inch length. Glue one end of an 18-inch length of pink picot ribbon to top back of heart, and wrap ribbon around heart through inside around outside until reaching the bottom. Spot-glue end to back to hold. Repeat with another 18-inch length for other half of heart. Tie a bow in the 12-inch length of pink picot ribbon and glue to top middle of heart.

4 Starting along the back top edge of the heart, apply a few inches of glue and place the binding edge of the 22-inch length of white lace, slightly gathering lace around curves.

5 For hanger loop, glue together ends of the remaining 10-inch length of pink picot ribbon and glue ends to back top of heart.

Patterns

(cut one unless noted)

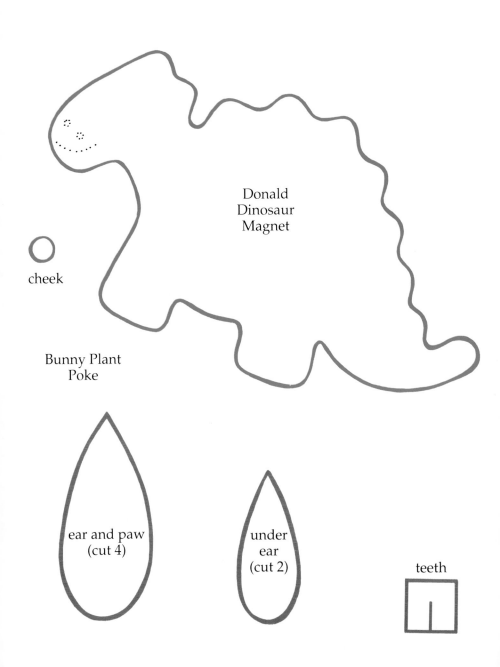

Donald
Dinosaur
Magnet

cheek

Bunny Plant
Poke

ear and paw
(cut 4)

under
ear
(cut 2)

teeth

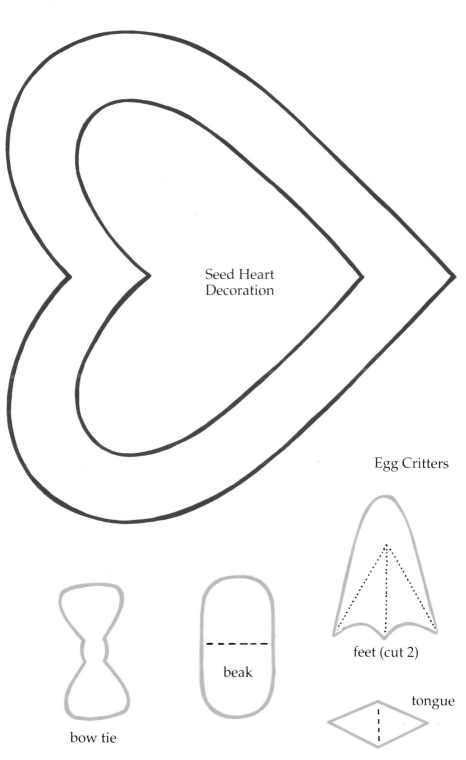

Seed Heart
Decoration

Egg Critters

feet (cut 2)

tongue

beak

bow tie

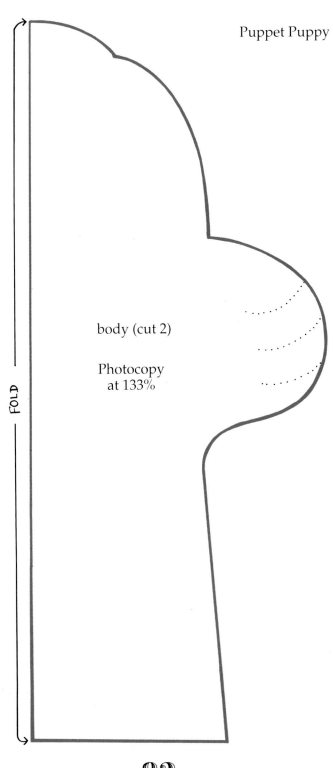

Puppet Puppy

FOLD

body (cut 2)

Photocopy
at 133%

82

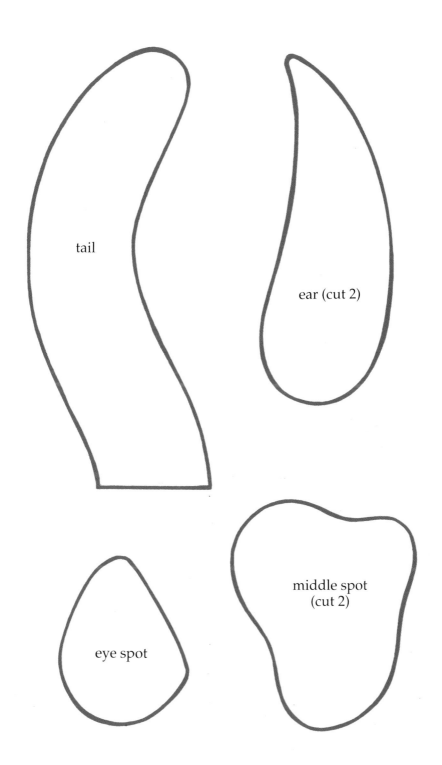

tail

ear (cut 2)

eye spot

middle spot
(cut 2)

Puppet Puppy

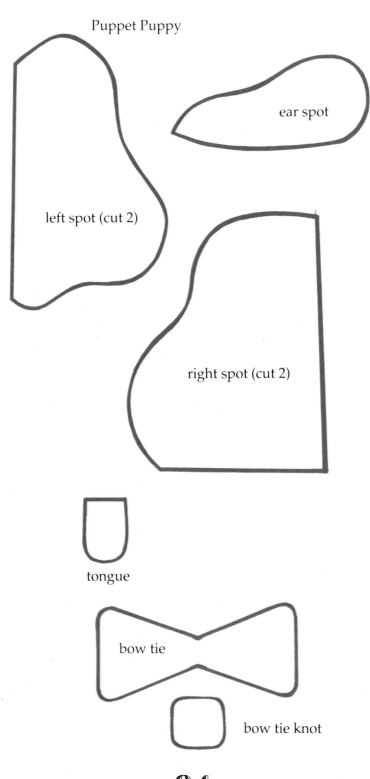

ear spot

left spot (cut 2)

right spot (cut 2)

tongue

bow tie

bow tie knot

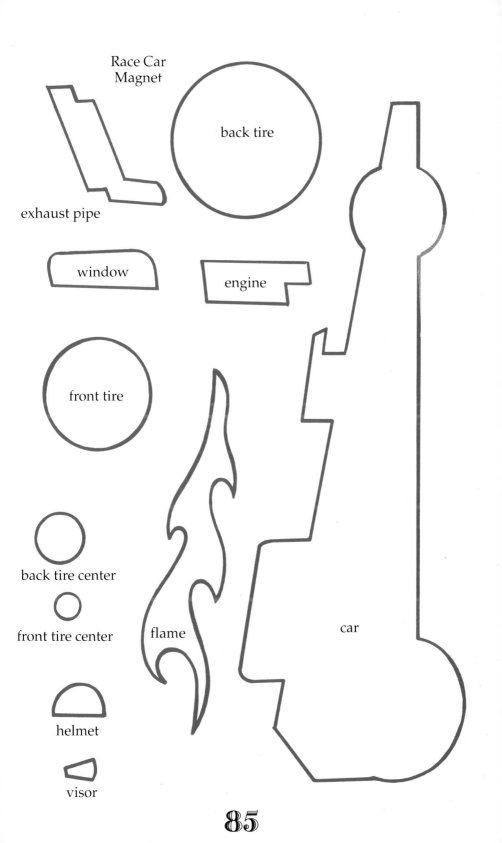

Race Car
Magnet

exhaust pipe

back tire

window

engine

front tire

back tire center

front tire center

flame

car

helmet

visor

85

Trick-or-Treat
Bag

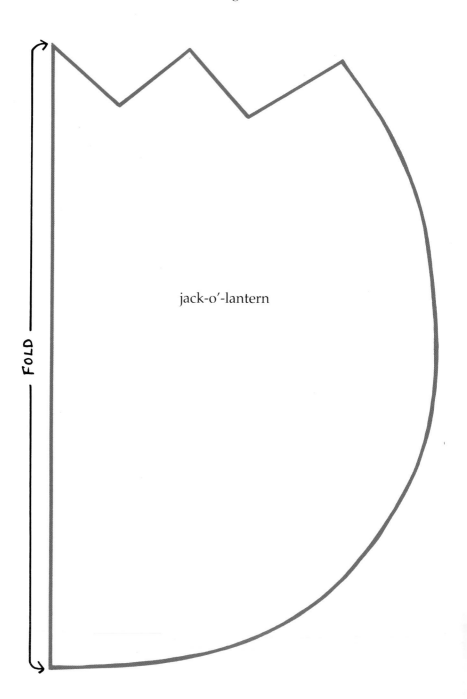

FOLD

jack-o'-lantern

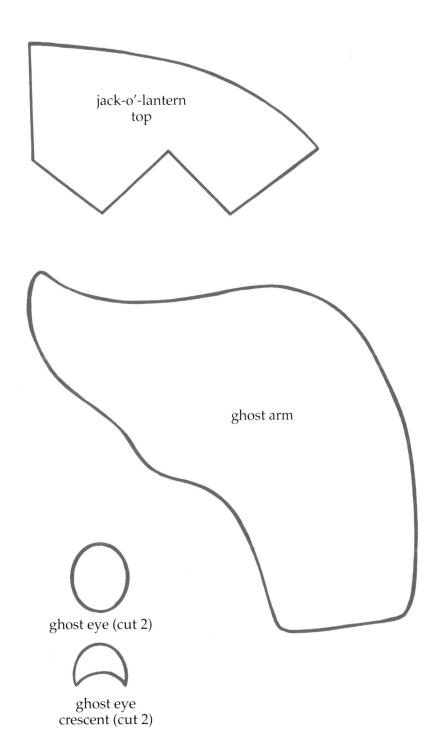

jack-o'-lantern
top

ghost arm

ghost eye (cut 2)

ghost eye
crescent (cut 2)

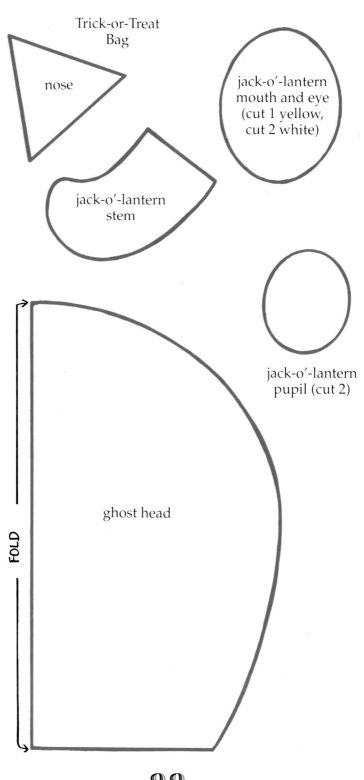

Trick-or-Treat
Bag

nose

jack-o'-lantern
mouth and eye
(cut 1 yellow,
cut 2 white)

jack-o'-lantern
stem

jack-o'-lantern
pupil (cut 2)

ghost head

FOLD

Doily Angel

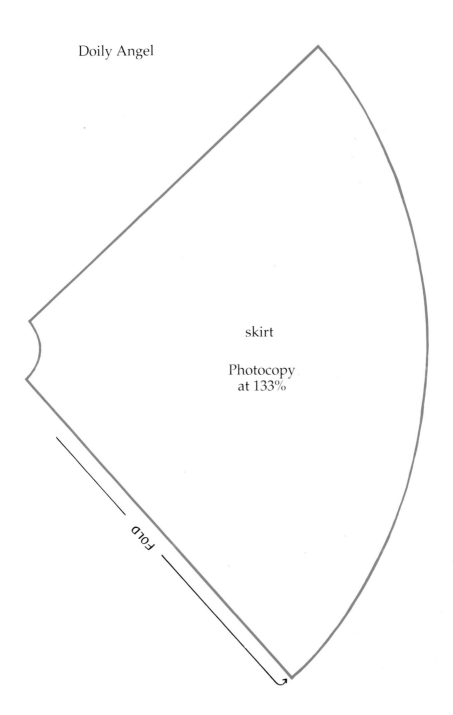

skirt

Photocopy
at 133%

FOLD

Doily Angel

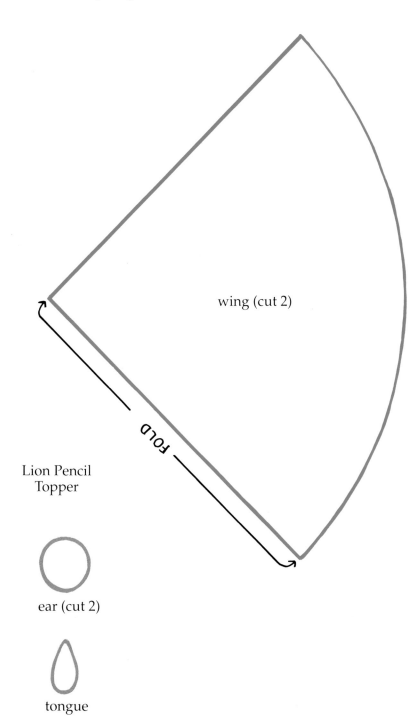

wing (cut 2)

FOLD

Lion Pencil Topper

ear (cut 2)

tongue

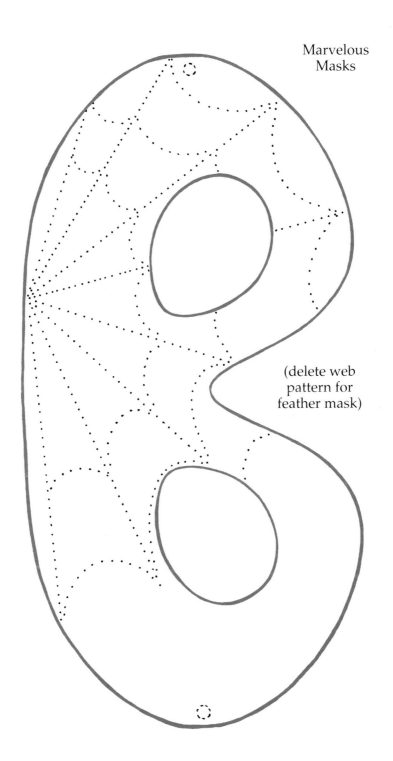

Marvelous
Masks

(delete web
pattern for
feather mask)

Petal Posies

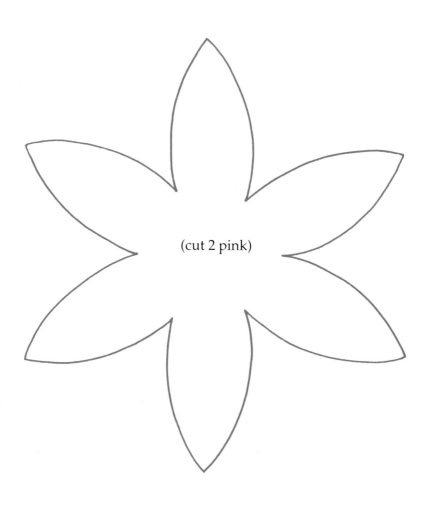

(cut 2 pink)

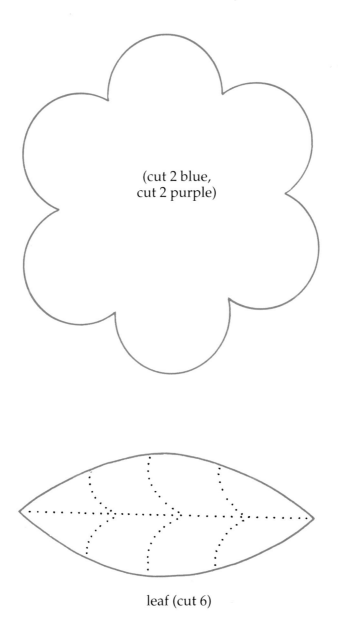

(cut 2 blue,
cut 2 purple)

leaf (cut 6)

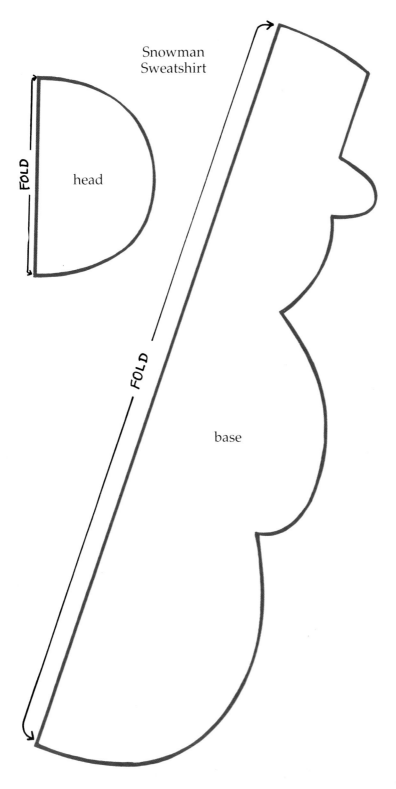

Snowman
Sweatshirt

head

FOLD

FOLD

base

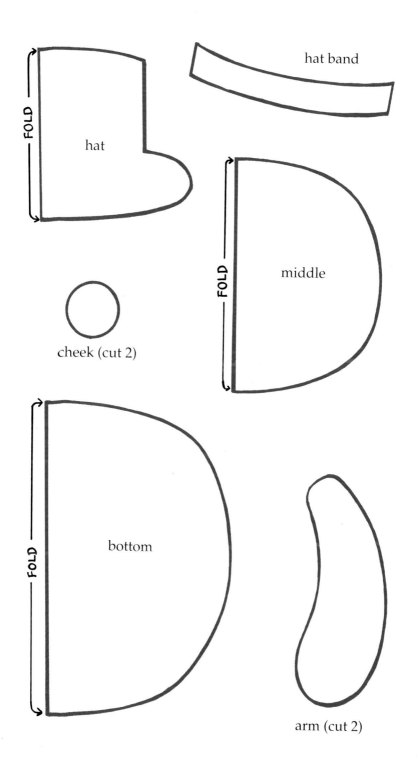

hat band

FOLD

hat

middle

FOLD

cheek (cut 2)

FOLD

bottom

arm (cut 2)

Soldier Magnet

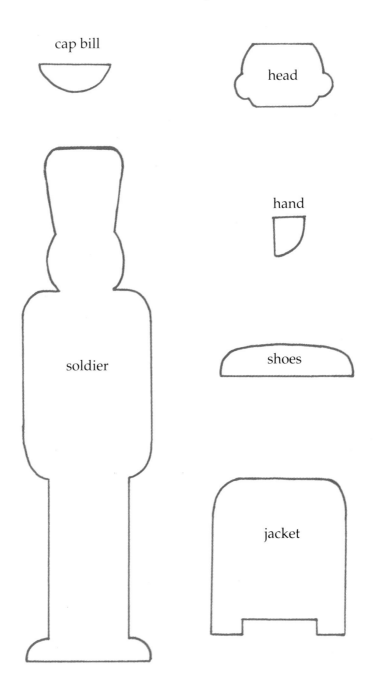

cap bill

head

hand

soldier

shoes

jacket